text
Kathleen Bowman

design concept
Larry Soule

photos
Globe: pp. 6, 18, 24, 28
UPI: pp. 12, 34, 36, 44

published by
Creative Education,
Mankato, Minnesota

ON STAGE ELVIS PRESLEY

Published by Creative Educational Society, Inc.,
123 South Broad Street, Mankato, Minnesota 56001
Copyright ® 1976 by Creative Educational Society, Inc. International
copyrights reserved in all countries.
No part of this book may be reproduced in any form without written
permission from the publisher. Printed in the United States.
Distributed by
Childrens Press, 1224 West Van Buren Street, Chicago, Illinois 60607
Library of Congress Numbers: 75-425-05   ISBN: 0-87191-488-3

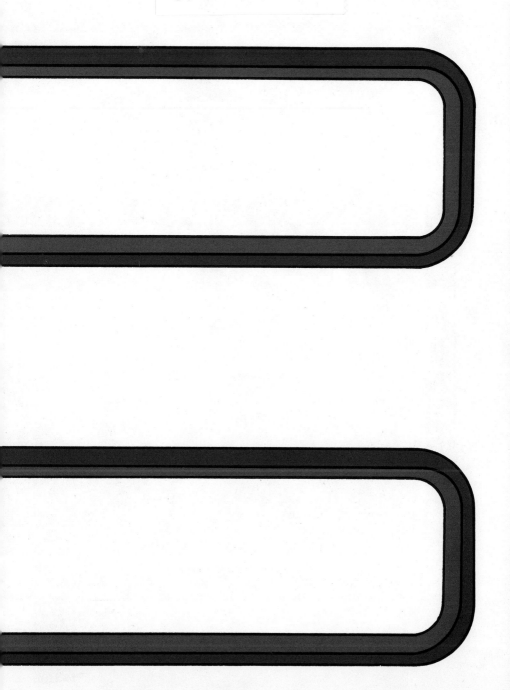

two songs for $4.00

One hot summer day in 1953, a lanky truck driver named Elvis Aron Presley parked his Ford pickup, pulled his battered guitar off the seat and strolled into the Memphis Recording Service. He'd passed the sign many times while making deliveries for a local electric company and finally saved enough money to record two songs for his mother's birthday.

The recording studio was busy that Saturday noon, and Elvis sat down to wait his turn, nervously running his hands through his collar-length hair. Marion Keisker, the office manager, asked him what kind of singer he was.

"I sing all kinds," Elvis replied.

"Who do you sound like?" she continued.

"I don't sound like nobody."

How right he was. Elvis Aron Presley hit the entertainment scene like a cyclone, stirring up controversy and altering the direction of popular music for all time.

The fifties were the days of bow-tied "crooners" whose sugary lyrics and droning melodies bored the growing teenage market. Then along came Presley — a punk kid with greasy hair, long sideburns, and a musical style that scandalized adults with its blunt lyrics and wild rhythms. Elvis moaned, groaned, shouted and sneered; in short, he used his wide-ranging baritone voice in any way necessary to convey his messages. And his quivering legs and swiveling hips raised the eyebrows of the older generation, earning him the nickname "Elvis the Pelvis."

But the teenagers idolized him, jamming concert halls where the frenzy rose until they ripped Elvis' pink shirts to ribbons and tore the shoes from his feet. "Presleymania" swept the land like an epidemic. Girls carved the name "Elvis" into their arms. Fans kicked through a plate glass door to get his autograph. Swooning teenagers were hospitalized after rock concerts. Souvenir-hunters snipped blades of grass from the singer's lawn.

Meanwhile, Elvis Presley's records sold by the millions. The titles rose regularly to the top of the charts and rolled off the tongues of disc jockeys: "Heartbreak Hotel," "Hound Dog," Don't Be Cruel," "Love Me Tender," "Any Way You Want Me." The lyrics spoke directly to the problems and experiences of the teenage listeners.

No one seemed to know just who the person was behind this spectacular phenomenon. But it didn't seem to matter. Popular music was never to be the same. For the dramatic story of Elvis Presley's rise to fame is also the story of the emergence of rock and roll.

Elvis Presley's first exposure to music was in the poverty-ridden town of Tupelo, Mississippi, where he was born on January 8, 1935. Tupelo was in the midst of the South's evangelical religious country, and the First Assembly of God Church provided a major influence on Presley's later style.

Elvis was immediately drawn to gospel music. As a small child, he would often slide off his mother's lap and run down the aisle to the altar. Mrs. Presley recalled, "He would stand looking up at the choir and try to sing with them. He was too little to know the words, of course, but he could carry the tune."

It was not only the choir, however, which captivated young Presley. During revivals the ministers dominated the service, calling out to the Lord, damning the Devil, and shaking as they prayed. Elvis observed that this highly emotional behavior had a much greater impact on the congregation than the choir: "There were these singers, perfectly fine singers, but nobody responded to them. Then there was the preachers and they cut up all over the place, jumpin' on the piano, movin' ever' which way. The audience liked 'em." Elvis drew upon both resources — learning the spiritual mode from the singers and the bodily movements and range of emotional expression from the preachers. In combination, they became the core of his style.

When Elvis was ten he got his first guitar — a $12.95 instrument that was the substitute for a bicycle that the Presleys could not afford. After two of his uncles showed him a few chords, Elvis taught himself to play by listening to the radio and copying what he heard. He spent hours absorbing popular country music by singers like Roy Acuff and Jimmie Rodgers. He also enjoyed listening to the black blues artists from the surrounding cotton country — Big Bill Broonzy, BB King, and Muddy Waters. Like no one before him, Elvis Presley began to synthesize the features of white fundamentalist spirituals, popular country songs, and black rhythm and blues.

When Elvis was thirteen, the Presleys moved to Memphis in search of jobs and better housing. Memphis was blues country, and Elvis continued to be haunted by the music the townsfolk called "sinful." No one could understand why a

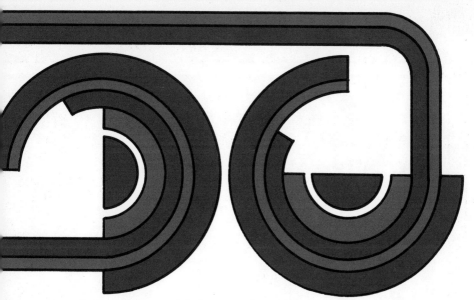

white boy could be so drawn to the raucous black music of Beale Street.

At Humes High School, Elvis played end on the football team. But his image was already beginning to set him apart from his fellow teenagers. One of his friends recalls, "Elvis had his hair real long . . . he was the only guy. The rest of us had crew cuts. I remember once when all the guys were gonna get him and cut his hair. I helped him escape from that."

Elvis also began dressing in loud color combinations, especially pink and black. He bought whatever clothing he could afford from a Beale Street store which was popular with Memphis blacks and Nashville country musicians. The store specialized in bright yellow suits and pink jackets decorated with glitter. Elvis was often harassed for his hair and his clothing, but no amount of antagonism seemed to shake his quiet confidence.

on record

By the time Elvis walked into the Memphis Recording Service that summer day in 1953, he had already developed a musical style and a personal image that were bound to attract attention.

Marion Keisker decided to listen in as Elvis began singing "My Happiness." Halfway through the song she hurriedly set up the taping system so her boss, Sam Phillips, could hear Elvis' voice.

Sam Phillips had often remarked, "If I could find a white man who had the Negro sound and the Negro feel, I could make a billion dollars." He was talking about "soul," and when Marion heard Elvis, she was certain that he had it.

When Sam heard the tape, he was impressed with the sound, but thought that Elvis needed work. The two men didn't meet until several months later, when Elvis came by the recording studio to cut a second record. Sam liked Elvis' performance on the two country ballads; he took down his name, address and a neighbor's phone number. The Presleys were too poor to afford a telephone.

For the next eight months Elvis continued to drive his delivery truck for $35 a week and waited for Sam Phillips to call. He sang every chance he got, usually at all-night gospel sings, backed by a quartet called the Songfellows.

One day Sam Phillips wanted to record a ballad but could not locate the young black singer who had done the demonstration record. Marion reminded him of Elvis: "What about the kid with the sideburns?"

Sam agreed to give him a try, and Marion put in the call to Presleys' neighbor. She recalls, "I was still standing there with the telephone in my hand and here comes Elvis, panting. I think he ran all the way."

Elvis' performance on the ballad was terrible, even though he tried again and again. Finally during a break Sam asked, "What can you do?"

"I can do anything." Elvis replied.

"Do it," said Sam.

So Elvis started singing everything he knew — gospel, pop, country-western, blues. Several hours later Sam decided to arrange a practice session for Elvis with Scotty Moore, a 21-year-old guitar player and Bill Black, a bass player.

One practice session turned into several months of rehearsals and hard work. Every day after work Scott, Bill and Elvis would meet in the tiny, cluttered Sun studio, trying to develop a style that would be unique.

Finally one night Sam decided he needed to see if they were all wasting their time on young

Presley. "Okay, this is the session," he announced, and headed for the control room. Elvis began with "I Love You Because," then sang a few country-style songs. They were all right, but nothing special.

Then during a break, while the musicians sat around drinking cokes, Elvis picked up his guitar and broke into "That's All Right Mama," a 1940's blues number sung originally by Big Boy Crudup. Elvis jumped around the studio while he sang, banging on his battered guitar. Soon Bill and Scotty joined the wild sound.

Sam came running out of the control room, shouting, "Don't lose it . . . let's put it on tape." The musicians' antics had created a sound far better than anything they had planned for the session. "That's All Right Mama" became Elvis Presley's first record.

And a famous record it was to become. Not only would it trigger Elvis Presley's climb to fame, but it would also set an important precedent in the history of American music. Elvis had merged the sounds of black rhythm and blues with white country music, creating what came to be called "rockabilly."

When the group heard themselves played back through the recording system, they thought, "They'll run us outa town when they hear it." No one was accustomed to mixing musical styles as they had done; radio stations played either "hillbilly" or "blues" — not both.

Sam Phillips decided to take the record to Dewey Phillips, a popular Memphis disc jockey and the only person Sam could think of who might consider playing it. Dewey himself mixed styles. Although he was white, he had a radio program on station WHBQ called "Red Hot and Blue," devoted to black blues singers. Dewey Phillips liked Elvis' record and agreed to play it on the air.

The night Elvis' songs were to be played, he was too nervous to listen. After tuning the family radio to WHBQ, he escaped to the darkness of his favorite movie theater.

But before long, Elvis' parents were roaming up and down the aisles trying to find him. Dewey Phillips had called and wanted to interview him. That night at the radio station the telephones had rung continuously in response to Elvis' record. By the time the show was over, Dewey Phillips had played the record 30 times.

When Elvis came running into the studio, Dewey said, "Sit down. I'm going to interview you."

"Mr. Phillips," Elvis protested, "I don't know nothing about being interviewed."

"Just don't say nothing dirty." Dewey warned him as he put on a couple of records. "I'll let you know when we're ready to start."

The two of them talked while the records played. Dewey asked Elvis what high school he had gone to, and he said "Humes." Dewey said later he wanted that on the air because many listeners had thought Elvis was black. It was a good indication of the genuine feel he gave to the blues.

Dewey finally said, "All right, Elvis, thank you very much."

"Aren't you gonna interview me?" Elvis inquired.

"I already have." said Dewey. "The mike's been open the whole time." Elvis broke out in a cold sweat.

18

long hard climb

By the end of July, 1954, "That's All Right" had appeared briefly in the number one position on charts in Memphis, New Orleans, and Nashville. **Billboard**, the country's top music magazine, hailed Elvis as "a potent new chanter who can sock over a tune for either the country or the rhythm and blues markets."

But success came slowly to Elvis. The record remained only a regional hit, and even in the South many copies of Elvis' first record went into trash cans instead of onto turntables. The U. S. Supreme Court had just banned racial segregation in the schools. White southerners were bitter, and the last thing they wanted to hear was a voice that sounded "integrated."

Presley's financial situation was not much better either. Sun Records was a small company and paid him infrequently.

Things appeared to be looking up when Elvis was invited to sing at the **Grand Ole Opry** in

Nashville. Few country singers were ever asked to appear at the famous show with only one record out, and singing at country music's version of Carnegie Hall could send Elvis into national fame. An excited group including Sam and Marion drove the four hours to Nashville with Elvis, Bill, and Scotty.

The afternoon of the show Elvis wandered around the 1892 building, distressed at its shabbiness. According to Marion, Elvis kept muttering, "You mean this is what I've been dreaming about all these years?"

For the performance Elvis sang two songs, "That's All Right" and "Blue Moon of Kentucky." When he walked off stage Jim Denny, the head of the **Opry's** talent office, told Elvis he should think about going back to driving a truck.

Elvis was devasted by the comment, but he refused to give up. Before long he got a booking on **Louisiana Hayride**, a radio program similar to **Grand Ole Opry**. His reception there was dramatically different. **Hayride's** drummer recalls the first night Elvis performed: "He was purty hot in the area anyway, and he tore the house down. . . . Horace Logan was the program director for the station and when Horace heard Elvis that first time, he did 14 back flips." Elvis was given a contract that made him one of the show's regulars.

The first time Elvis began to evoke hysteria in an audience was at an all-country music show in the Overton Park Shell in Memphis. Elvis' afternoon show, filled with country ballads, had not drawn much reaction from the crowd. So Dewey Phillips, the disc jockey, told Elvis to forget the ballads and sing "Good Rockin' Tonight." Elvis shook and gyrated with the fast rhythm of the song, and the evening audience went wild. It was a sign of things to come.

Elvis' career remained regional and only moderately successful until a man named Colonel Tom Parker entered his life in February, 1955.

"The Colonel," as he was called, had been a carnival promoter; long before he came upon Elvis he had learned to use his shrewd style to sell the public just about anything. Once he'd even painted sparrows yellow and sold them as canaries to gullible carnival visitors.

His keen ability to recognize a good bet told him he couldn't miss on Elvis. He made his initial connection by helping Elvis' first manager, Bob Neal, with bookings in the South and Southwest. And he kept his eye on the record charts and audience reactions to the up-and-coming star.

The Colonel's strategy for obtaining Elvis was to convince his parents that he should be Elvis' manager. He invited Vernon Presley to a series of "policy meetings" discussing Elvis' plans and suggested that the singer leave Sun Records. Once he'd convinced Elvis' father, the Colonel went to his mother. He told her, "You got the finest boy in the world, Miz Presley, and it's terrible the way they're makin' him work." He gave the Presleys $200 and told them to send Elvis up to his farm to relax. Before long, the Colonel had a long telegram in his hand giving him the power to find a buyer for Elvis Presley. It was signed by his parents.

The Colonel sold Elvis' contract to RCA Victor for $35,000, an enormous sum by 1955 standards. RCA agreed to promote the young star in all three music fields: country, pop, and rhythm and blues.

In his last months with Sun Records, Elvis had made several more discs: "I'm Left, You're Right, She's Gone," "Mystery Train," and "Baby, Let's Play House." This last song was the first Elvis Presley record to appear on national best-

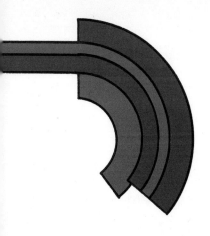

seller charts. It was a blues number, introducing the hiccuping sound which became an Elvis trademark. The other songs were country western.

But by the time of Elvis' first RCA recording session, his style had undergone some changes. Scotty Moore's hard driving country guitar sound was gone, as well as the "boogie beat." Elvis was turning increasingly to a ballad style with a piano background. This change appealed directly to the growing pop audience, instead of to listeners who like rockabilly. The Colonel, no doubt, encouraged these changes, looking to the increased profits from a wider audience appeal. As the appeal broadened, however, Elvis grew increasingly distant from the folk roots of his music.

No one paid this much heed. "Heartbreak Hotel" had been a smashing national success and television programmers were competing for the star. Elvis was on his way.

controversy

Meanwhile, the country rocked with emotion over Elvis, ranging from adoration to outrage. As the teenagers' shrieks grew louder, so did parents' indignant responses. Elvis' appearances on television brought his swiveling hips and flamboyant outfits right into the living rooms of countless American families, escalating the conflict.

Forgetting their own parents' hostile reactions to jazz in the 1930's, adults in the 1950's proclaimed Elvis' performances in bad taste and worried that he would corrupt teenagers. A group of women from Syracuse, New York, sent petitions to three networks asking that Elvis be barred from television. The City Council of San Antonio removed all rock and roll records from swimming pool juke boxes to prevent swimmers from practicing "spastic gyrations" in time to the music. Many cities prohibited rock concerts altogether, and the **New York Daily News** proposed that teenagers be forbidden to dance in public unless they had a signed note from their parents!

But the criticism extended also to Elvis' singing ability. Some said he had absolutely no talent

— that he did nothing but whine and mumble and cover his mistakes with wiggling behavior and wild costumes. It annoyed some music critics that someone they thought to be such a fraud could own three Cadillacs and be making over $7,500 a week.

Even fellow country musicians turned against Elvis. Many of them despised what they saw as contamination of country music with other influences. Most of all they hated Elvis' spectacular popularity because it adversely affected their own record sales.

By the time Elvis was drafted into the Army in 1957, the Colonel's strategy had shifted. This change became clear when officials offered Elvis a job in Special Services entertaining the troops. The singing star refused, not wanting to take the easy way out.

The Colonel strongly encouraged Presley's inclination for several reasons. First, he did not want Elvis ever to sing without pay. Secondly, he did not want Elvis to be accused of receiving favorite treatment. That would be bad publicity. The Colonel was so concerned about the favoritism issue that he wouldn't allow Elvis to sing at the General's daughter's birthday party unless every soldier in Elvis' unit was invited! Finally, the Colonel shrewdly perceived that the older generation would accept Elvis once he had demonstrated his ability to be a regular soldier in the U. S. Army. The initial controversy had served its purpose — Elvis was famous. Now the Colonel wanted to win over still one more group of potential buyers in his grand scheme.

The Colonel proved himself right again. By the time Elvis got out of the Army with his crew cut and sergeant's stripes, he had won the approval of most adults. The Mississippi State Legislature went so far as to pass a resolution stating that Elvis had become "a legend and an inspiration to tens of millions of Americans." In addition, Senator Estes Kefauver of Tennessee placed a tribute to Elvis in the **Congressional Record**. Elvis Presley's appeal now spanned two generations of Americans.

rock bottom

Ultimately the brand of success that the Colonel manufactured for Elvis took its toll on both the fans and the performer. From the beginning, according to many observers, the Colonel regarded Elvis more as a product than a person. He seemed consumed by the desire to make money and gave Presley little opportunity to direct his own career. Colonel Tom Parker told Elvis when, where, and often how to sing and make movies; decided precisely how much he would earn; and even spoke for him in interviews. Except for recordings and concerts, Elvis remained in the background.

And there seemed to be no limit to the kinds of techniques Parker would use to sell his "product." He inserted what was supposedly a scrap of Elvis' clothing in each of the first 150,000 copies of an LP; he rented elephants and midgets to advertise Elvis; and he flooded the market with countless items of merchandise with Elvis' name — bobbysocks, purses, jeans, belts, hairbrushes, stationery.

The Colonel, of course, knew what he was doing. First, by keeping the public's access to Elvis limited to a few performances, he created a high level of demand in fans for some kind of connection to the star. He then met that demand by feeding merchandise to people who were so starved for knowledge of the real Elvis they would accept almost anything as a substitute. Elvis had become, many say, a commercial image defined and manipulated by the Colonel.

The tight control on the celebrity eventually affected his performance. Perhaps it was not only the fans who did not know the real Elvis; perhaps Elvis himself came to rely too heavily on the Colonel's version of him.

In any case, during the nine years after Elvis left the Army, through the 1960's, Elvis did not seem to be making use of his wide-ranging talents as an actor and singer. The pressure to sell himself to the widest possible audience diluted his style from a unique, spontaneous phenomenon to one which became increasingly bland and ill-defined.

Then, caught in the grip of several Hollywood contracts negotiated by the Colonel, Elvis starred in a string of 21 movies at a rate of three per year. There was little time to concentrate on quality, so a series of shallow, mediocre films resulted. Any deliberation during the shooting of the films was over such questions as whether or not Elvis should wear brown contact lenses over his blue eyes. Yet despite the unrealistic, predictable quality to the movies, loyal fans mobbed the theaters; it was their only chance to see Elvis, who did no concerts or interviews during this period.

Elvis grew frustrated with his own work. This was not his style of producing material. On the contrary, Elvis had always been a perfectionist. An RCA producer once recalled: "We would make a lot of takes and we would get to the point where I thought we had a pretty good one. And I'd say, 'I think we got it pretty good there, Elvis.' And he would say, 'I think I can do a little better.'" And he would try it again. With this kind of desire to work hard for even minimal improvements, it is little wonder that Elvis soon grew bitter at the speed with which the films had to be cranked out. After one of the MGM films had been completed, Elvis walked over to the director and said, "Hey, there were some pretty funny things in this script. I'm gonna have to read it someday."

Many actors working with Elvis were impressed with his potential, as were many of his directors. Joe Pasternak said, "Elvis should be given more meaty parts . . . he's got guts, he's got strength, he's got charm. . . . He should do more important pictures."

But Elvis, perhaps because his life had been run for so long by someone else, seemed powerless to make decisions about the use of his own talent. He stagnated; even his most ardent supporters stopped going to Elvis' films. And for several years he was utterly unable to come up with a number one record.

comeback

In 1968, the Colonel arranged for Elvis to do an hour-long live Christmas special for NBC-TV. Steve Binder, the producer and director, recognized the show as Elvis' "moment of truth." Steve knew that if Elvis did a show that was like his movies, he would be finished. On the other hand, an exciting show could trigger a comeback for the fallen star.

The night of the special, Elvis was so nervous that his hand shook the microphone. But once he began singing, Elvis performed with a vitality and charisma that seemed to surpass even the best of his early shows. He sang dozens of old hits with naturalness and spontaneity, sweating and moving with the music in the bright spotlights.

For the first time, he laughed and talked and contributed his own unrehearsed lines, and he closed the show with "If I Can Dream" — a song written especially for Elvis by Earl Brown. It was a plea for peace and understanding that became Elvis' first million seller in over three years.

The critics raved about about Elvis, commenting on his lack of pretension, his commitment, and his power to involve the audience. A

reporter wrote, "There is something magical about watching a man who has lost himself find his way back home."

Everyone wondered what Elvis would do next. Would he make 25 more bad movies? To that frequent question Elvis replied, "No, no I won't. I'm going to do things now." It seemed that Elvis had found himself again.

And he was a man of his word. In January, 1969, he returned to Memphis after a 14-year absence. Many people saw it as a symbolic move — that Elvis was "going home" to the roots of his music.

Elvis was tired of hearing his voice on movie sound tracks and wanted to get back to a more original style. For 10 days and nights Elvis worked in the studio, cutting enough material to produce more than two long-playing albums. In a phenomenally productive recording session, he belted out country songs, rhythm and blues, and ballads. "In the Ghetto," a protest song released as a single, became Elvis' first gold record since 1961.

Finally, in the summer of 1969, Elvis began rehearsing for his first public appearance in almost nine years. The excitement mounted as opening night grew near. Could Elvis draw the crowds? Would he have his old appeal?

Las Vegas' Showroom Internationale was packed that August evening. Fans had come from

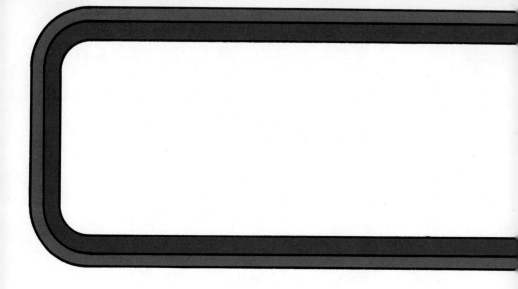

as far away as Europe and Australia, and Hollywood celebrities eagerly awaited the return of the superstar. Suddenly, the orchestra exploded into the "Theme from 2001," and a radiant Elvis Presley bounded to center stage. His tan face beamed with confidence and he was stunningly dressed in a pure white buckskin jumpsuit cut to the waist.

The crowd went wild — stomping, whistling, shrieking, and clamoring onto tables and chairs for a better view of the famous performer who had been hidden from view for almost a decade.

Grabbing the microphone, Elvis broke into "Blue Suede Shoes," his legs vibrating and knees snapping with the driving beat of the guitars: "Waaal, it's one for the money/Two for the show/Three to get ready, now go cat, go . . ."

Elvis was back. Not the punk kid with greasy hair, dressed in a pink sport coat, but a versatile

and grown-up performer, comfortable with himself at last.

Elvis, too, seemed aware of the change. He sang a medley of old hits with a touch of humor, seemingly laughing at his old image of "Hound-Dog" days. Then he sang "Yesterday" and "Hey, Jude," Beatles' songs. At this important moment Elvis brought together on that Las Vegas stage two of the most important influences in the history of rock and roll. Years before, Elvis had been an inspiration for the Beatles when they were poor English youths; now they were an inspiration for Elvis as he renewed his own career.

The ecstatic crowd gave Elvis several standing ovations, and the critics raved, calling him "unbelievable," "supernatural," and "one of the most powerful acts in Vegas history."

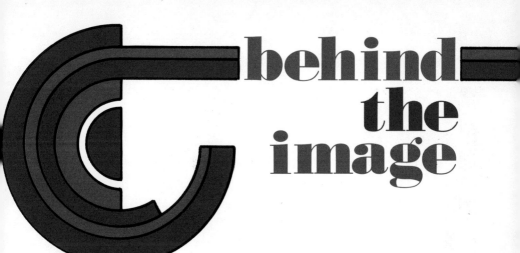

behind the image

Today, the King of Rock and Roll works only about two months out of the year — usually in Las Vegas, with one or two appearances elsewhere. These box office earnings, plus the profit from record sales and publishing royalties, give him an annual income of about 5 million dollars.

Despite this wealth, Elvis retains many of the "down-home" traits of his earlier, leaner years. As always, he is extremely close to his family and a tightly knit circle of friends. His ex-wife Priscilla and daughter Lisa Marie live in California, but Elvis sees them often. His father Vernon, his stepmother, and three stepbrothers live adjacent to Graceland, Elvis' Memphis estate. So do his grandmother, two uncles and an aunt. And most of the people on his personal payroll are relatives or friends of long-standing.

Elvis' generosity is legendary. His Uncle Travis often tells the story of the time Elvis drove

41

one of his new pickup trucks down to check the progress of a man repairing a fence on the estate.

"Shore do like that truck. Always wanted me one of them," the man said.

"You got a dollar?" Elvis asked. The man handed a dollar to Elvis.

"It's your truck," Elvis said, and walked away.

Elvis' friends are frequently the recipients of lavish gifts from the star — often Cadillacs and motorcycles. If someone admires one of Elvis' possessions, he is likely to give it away.

Because Elvis has played so many shallow movie roles, many people have underestimated his intelligence. But actors who have worked with him are quick to defend Elvis' brightness and curiosity. Stan Brossette, for example, notes Elvis' fascination with the meaning of words: "He'll ask what a word means: 'Say it again . . . can you use it this way, that way?' His mind is so fine, so sharp, he could have been anything he wanted." Elvis' eagerness to learn, combined with irrepressible energy and a keen sense of humor, are among the factors which have helped sustain Elvis through an astounding career that now spans two generations of admirers.

And his fans today are no less devoted than the teenagers of the 1950's. According to Tom

Parker's offices, there are some 3,000 Elvis fan clubs in existence today, and Elvis very likely continues to be the single entertainment personality with the largest number of admirers. Many of these people work in order to buy tickets to Memphis, where they camp out at Graceland hoping for a glimpse of Presley. One woman said, "I think being an Elvis fan is like being in love. You can't explain **why** or **how** it happened, but that feeling is just there and unmistakable."

Not all Elvis fans are women. A 28-year-old construction worker from the East has named two children for Elvis. One is "Stephen Elvis" and the other is "Lonnie Glen" — Lonnie from the film **Tickle Me** and Glen from **Wild in the Country**. In Maryland, a policeman corresponds with other Elvis fans in Japan, Italy, and England as well as keeping a detailed set of statistics on all aspects of Presley. He claims to have one of the most complete Elvis Presley collections in the world.

That Elvis continues to be a favorite with the public can be seen in the volume of merchandise an Oregon college student sells. He can hardly keep up with the orders; items include bumper stickers, T-shirts, combs, and stamps. The pencils which are for sale read, "FOREVER KING ELVIS."

Twenty years after his entrance onto the entertainment scene, the debate about Elvis Presley is far from over. Today, no one argues about whether he has talent, as people did in the 1950's. The star's abilities are unquestioned. The current debate is over whether or not Elvis Presley's potential is being creatively challenged.

Some critics argue that the Colonel once again has Elvis as his captive — this time in Las Vegas nightclubs, instead of Hollywood studios. The claim the Colonel has transformed Elvis into a plastic puppet who makes money by flattering rich middle-aged women. At the same time, they feel he has abandoned the kinds of audiences that originally brought him fame.

And who is this star they describe? He has lavish costumes, a bland, syrupy singing style, and an overpowering back-up of singing groups and twenty-three piece orchestras. This is a far cry, they say, from the revival stage style that made Elvis an unusual and powerful musical

phenomenon. Presley is too polished and too rehearsed. The accuse him of selling-out to the show biz establishment.

Many Elvis admirers, ranging from fans who were teenagers in the 1950's to present day hippies, are angry with the Colonel's manipulation of Elvis; they claim that the star's talent can and should transcend the Las Vegas glitter. These fans long for the colorful Elvis of his early career, singing raw, gutsy blues and raunchy country songs. In those days he drew on the rich traditions of spirituals, slave songs, and hillbilly ballads.

It is impossible to say which Elvis will prevail. Throughout his career he has remained a mysterious and elusive personality. But regardless of the direction his future takes, certain staggering accomplishments ensure him a prominent spot in the history of popular culture.

Almost singlehandedly, Elvis developed the type of music we call "rock and roll," synthesizing the previously distinct styles of country western, rhythm and blues, and pop. Moreover, he was the first rock artist in history to become a popular hero in foreign countries and to have an independent movie career. And he remains the biggest record-selling artist of all time. It is fitting then that the **London Times** placed Elvis Aron Presley on its list of people who helped shape the twentieth century.